CUMBRIA LIBRARIES

3 8003 03520 7448

KU-031-104

Penrith Library

HADRIAN'S WALL

DERRY BRABBS

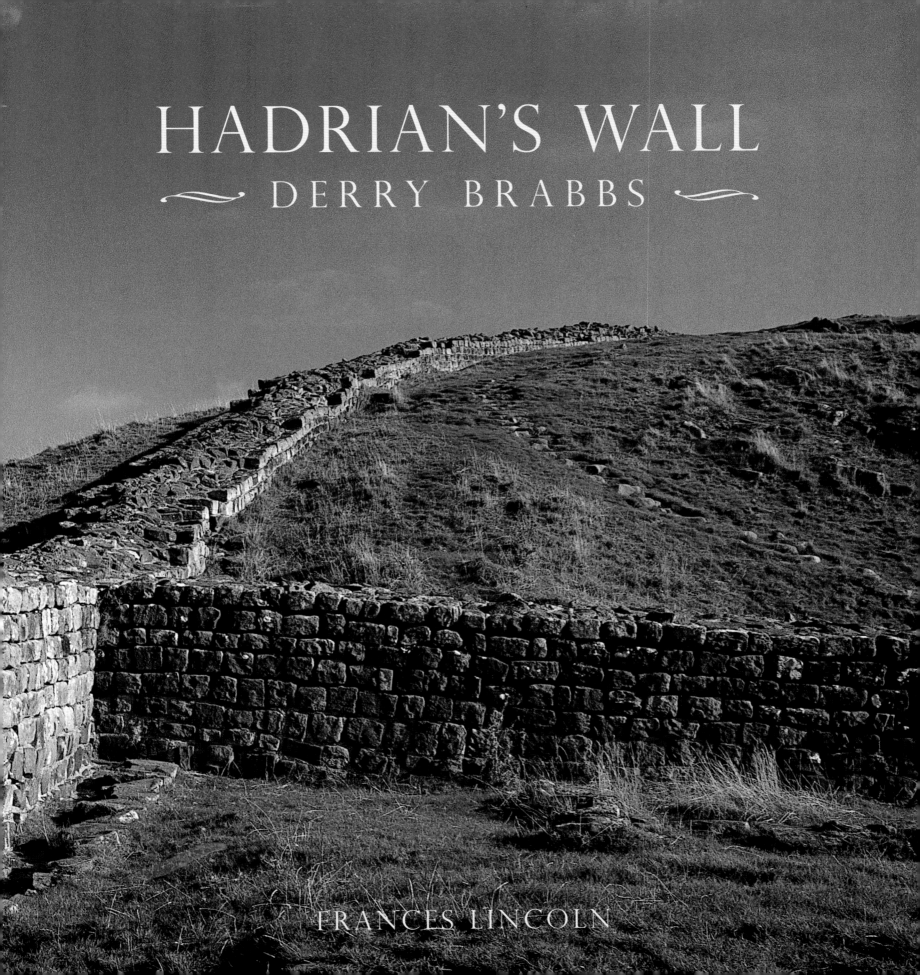

HADRIAN'S WALL

⊰ DERRY BRABBS ⊱

FRANCES LINCOLN

Frances Lincoln Limited
4 Torriano Mews
Torriano Avenue
London NW5 2RZ

Hadrian's Wall
Copyright © 2008 Frances Lincoln Limited

Text and photographs copyright © 2008 Derry Brabbs
Edited and designed by Jane Havell Associates

First Frances Lincoln edition published in the UK
and the USA 2008

Derry Brabbs has asserted his moral right to be identified
as Author of this Work in accordance with the Copyright,
Designs and Patents Act 1988

All rights reserved. No part of this publication may be
reproduced, stored in a retrieval system or transmitted, in any
form, or by any means, electronic, mechanical, photocopying,
recording or otherwise, without either prior permission in
writing from the publishers or a licence permitting restricted
copying. In the United Kingdom such licences are issued by the
Copyright Licensing Agency, Saffron House, 6–10 Kirby Street,
London EC1N 8TS

British Library cataloguing-in-publication data
A catalogue record for this book is available from
the British Library

ISBN 978 0 7112 2857 3

Printed and bound in Singapore

9 8 7 6 5 4 3 2 1

Grateful thanks are due to my indefatigable editor and
designer, Jane Havell; to English Heritage, Tyne & Wear
Museums and the Museum of Antiquities, Newcastle upon
Tyne, for allowing me to take photographs on their properties,
and to Emperor Hadrian for creating such a fabulously
photogenic subject!

*Title pages: the south gate of Milecastle 39 (also known as Castle
Nick), the impressive remains of which lie sheltered in a hollow
of the Whin Sill.*

*Opposite: a modern statue representing Emperor Hadrian
celebrates Brampton's historic links to the Roman Wall.*

◠ Contents

Introduction ⌐✦

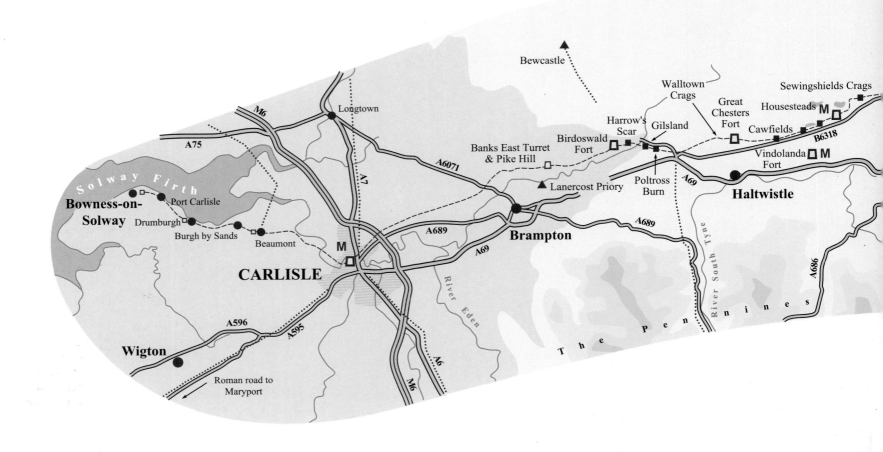

Hadrian's Wall is arguably the most important extant monument dating from the Roman Empire, built in 122 AD on the orders of Emperor Hadrian (ruled 117–38) to secure and control the Empire's northernmost border. It cleverly utilised the narrowest part of the land mass, extending for some 117 kilometres across the Tyne–Solway isthmus, the trim geographic waistline that conveniently divides the mainland into virtually two equal halves.

The Wall was designated a UNESCO World Heritage Site in 1987. In 2005 it was reclassified, together with the German 'Limes' (part of a barrier extending down the Rhine and Danube which performed a similar function) as 'The Frontiers of the Roman Empire'. These fortified borders along the northern and eastern European provinces were part of an elaborate frontier system which, at the

apogee of the Empire's power and extent in the early second century, extended for nearly 5,000 kilometres.

Many countries possess more aesthetically pleasing architectural legacies from that era (such as the sublimely beautiful city of Leptis Magna in Libya), but few come close to matching Hadrian's Wall in terms of its reflection of the power exerted over the 'civilised world' by the might of the Roman Empire. The bleak hills and wide expanses of Northumberland are a far cry from the sun-drenched Mediterranean sites normally associated with Ancient Rome: an isolation that makes the achievement of those who planned and constructed the Wall an even greater triumph of civil and military engineering than it would have been under more benign conditions.

While this volume is not intended as a guidebook, the linear nature of Hadrian's Wall does lend itself to

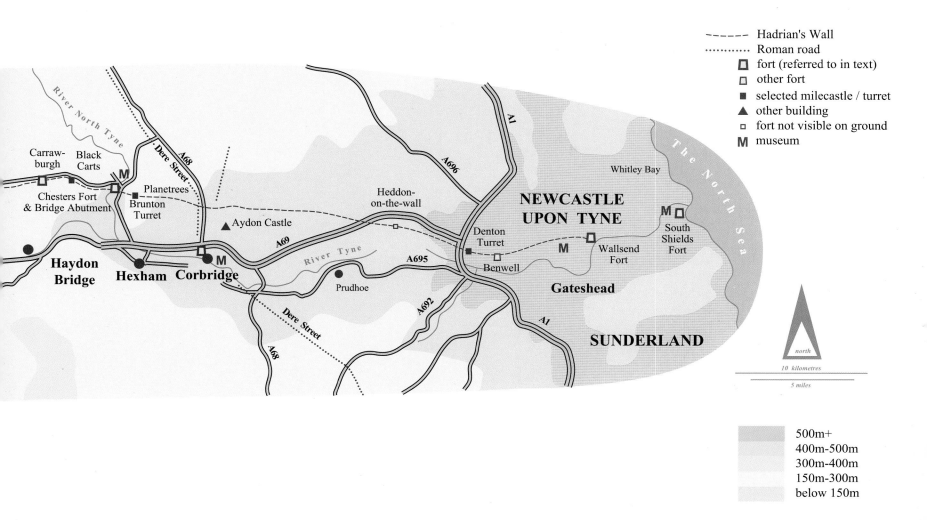

------ Hadrian's Wall
········ Roman road
□ fort (referred to in text)
▯ other fort
■ selected milecastle / turret
▲ other building
▫ fort not visible on ground
M museum

500m+
400m-500m
300m-400m
150m-300m
below 150m

Overleaf: the Stanegate fort of Vindolanda has yielded many important discoveries, such as writing tablets, still legible today, on which the soldiers left lists, notes and drafts of letters home. Now in the British Museum, they have added greatly to our knowledge about everyday life on Hadrian's Wall.

starting at one end and finishing at the other – and that is what I have done! The map above clearly highlights the route of the Wall, its proximity to the current road network and where the most important sites are located. A National Trail long-distance footpath, the Hadrian's Wall Path, was formally opened in 2003; its dedicated 'step by step' pocket guide takes walkers from east to west. I have opted to travel in the opposite direction, however, for two basic reasons. It seems more logical to finish, rather than start, the journey at a place called Wallsend. Perhaps more importantly, it is far easier and more comfortable to walk with the prevailing wind and weather on one's back, rather than battling head-on against it.

Exploring Hadrian's Wall by car has the obvious benefit of enabling people to reach widely spread locations with a minimum of fuss, whereas the walker is limited to appreciating whatever sites happen to be encompassed within the duration of a day's expedition. However, having made ample use of both modes of transport, I can confirm that pedestrians sometimes fare better than motorists along certain sections of the Wall, because the B6318 is almost totally devoid of safe places to stop (other than the designated car parks allied to major sites). Consequently, the notion of pulling over to admire or photograph an eye-catching view is not something I would recommend.

Inevitably, there are stretches where no tangible remains survive. But even in those places where the Wall may have disappeared from sight, it nevertheless survives in the many churches, farms and manor houses whose own solid walls bear testimony to its presence over almost two thousand years.

1 Background & History

When one considers the sheer size and scale of the Roman Empire during the first and second centuries AD, a small group of islands whose southern coastline was just visible across the English Channel could well have been deemed a superfluous trifle; scarcely worth the hazard and expense of a sea-borne invasion simply for the sake of adding another province to an already burgeoning and diverse international portfolio. Although the Province the Romans named Britannia did eventually become an important trading partner and contributor to the Empire's economy, it could just as easily have remained as it was, an island rich in natural resources that had been successfully and productively settled by Celtic tribes. Many Romans perceived Britain as a remote, barbaric place but traders from other Mediterranean countries had been conducting business there for many years prior to the first of Julius Caesar's two incursions in 55 BC.

Despite returning with five legions after the previous year's failure to progress much further inland than the south coast, Caesar still did not necessarily view the 54 BC landings as an attempt to overpower the Celtic tribes and establish a formal administration – it was more an opportunity to boost his own personal kudos. His army fought its way up to and across the River Thames into what is now Hertfordshire, overcoming tenacious resistance from some tribes, but the Romans were also aided by intelligence from others who placed a higher priority on internecine squabbles than on repelling a foreign invader. Caesar finally achieved the surrender of Cassivellaunus, king of the powerful Catuvellauni, took hostages from some tribes, set up alliances with others and was thus able to return home in triumph.

During the following decades, trade and cultural links with the Roman Empire increased, although bitter tribal rivalry persisted to such an extent that some groups actually sought help from Rome: requests arrived not long after the surprise accession of Claudius as emperor (r. 41–54 AD) in the confusing aftermath of the assassination of Caligula. Retaining one's position as emperor during those turbulent times required both staunch allies within Rome and military success in the far-flung corners of an expanding empire, a brief that could be met perfectly by a full-scale invasion of Britain.

Claudius elected not to lead the army himself but appointed Aulus Plautius as his commander-in-chief. The Roman force of some 40,000 troops and auxiliaries landed safely at Richborough in Kent and moved rapidly northwards, engaging the Britons in a

Opposite: the Roman lighthouse (pharos) still stands within the walls of Dover Castle in Kent. It was one of two built to guide troops and supplies safely across the English Channel to the Roman Empire's final and most northerly acquisition.

11

two-day battle near the River Medway. Further advances were swift: several tribes, especially those with trading connections, welcomed the Romans, while others accepted the futility of resistance.

Once the dust of battle had settled, Claudius duly arrived from Gaul to claim the spoils of victory at a magnificent ceremony staged in Camulodunum (near Colchester), where he received the formal submission of several British tribal chiefs. In a show of arrogant bravado, the emperor had shipped several elephants across the Channel to accompany his procession, and those great animals must have presented an awesome and intimidating spectacle. The new rulers were quick to consolidate their position, drawing upon their highly disciplined and effective legionaries to construct forts, bridges and roads.

However, although many tribes accepted the new status quo, others were less willing to yield to the invaders. While initially offering fierce resistance, they were essentially outfought by a superior and far more heavily armed force. The greatest uprising did not take place until seventeen years after the invasion, the catalyst for it being the death of Prasutagas, chief of the East Anglian Iceni tribe. As Prasutagas had no sons and the Romans did not recognise female accession, they took all his land, goods and posses-

Above left: a mid-nineteenth-century bronze statue of Boudica and her daughters on the London Embankment. Dramatically portrayed in her war-chariot, the queen of the Iceni tribe became an iconic symbol of Britain's dogged determination in the face of oppression.

Above right: in Wheeldale Moor in North Yorkshire, a mile-long stretch of Roman road has been stripped of its top dressing but retains its hard-core base and original flanking drainage channels.

sions, flogged his wife Boudica and raped their two daughters.

Such violent and unwarranted actions were, understandably, met with outrage by the Iceni. They joined forces with another tribe, the Trinovantes, and exacted a terrible revenge upon both the occupiers and any hapless citizens who happened to be in their way. It is estimated that the bloodletting cost in the region of 70,000 lives, the violence going largely unchecked because the Legions were campaigning against the Druids in Anglesey and North Wales. When the inevitable showdown happened, the tribal forces were defeated; Boudica took poison rather than face capture, torture and more humiliation.

Although harsh reprisals followed the Iceni revolt, a gradual return to a more conciliatory regime saw the colonised regions of Britannia begin to settle down. Prosperity was centred predominantly in the south and east of the country, northern tribes such as the Brigantes having proved significantly less sanguine about having to learn Latin than their southern neighbours! Civil war in Rome diverted attention away from subduing the north of the Province, but the Brigantes were finally defeated near what is now Scotch Corner on the A1, formerly the Roman highway of Dere Street.

Right: Dere Street, near Piercebridge, Co. Durham, was one of Roman Britain's major roads, running from York to the Firth of Forth. From Corbridge and the Wall, the modern A68 trunk road has adopted its course up to Scotland.

During those nationwide campaigns, efficient movement of men and materials over long distances was made possible by a rapidly expanding road network. The work was carried out by disciplined and versatile legionaries, supplemented by a conscripted local labour force. All roads were kept as straight as possible through meticulous surveying, a feat not always achievable on the more inhospitable terrain of upland England. A gravelled surface on a solid flag or rock base ensured the swift and safe movement of men and horses, reflecting the strategic military functions for which the roads were designed.

Much of the campaigning undertaken in Wales, the far north of England and Scotland was conducted during the governorship of General Julius Agricola (served 77–84 AD). Once the northern sector was made safer, the Romans were able actively to harvest the region's rich mineral deposits, expanding the road network in the process, and also building a succession of forts to protect their interests. The Brigantes and their allies may have been temporarily subdued, but the rough terrain of the Pennines and Northumberland provided perfect cover for anyone wishing to mount a guerrilla campaign, and the Romans took few chances when protecting the Empire's assets.

Main roads such as Dere Street ran roughly from

north to south, and a major lateral route known as the Stanegate was also established between Newcastle, Corbridge and Carlisle. The Stanegate runs roughly parallel to the line later adopted by Hadrian's Wall; having been well fortified along much of its length, it might have temporarily acted as a nominal frontier zone. Agricola and the Legions pressed ever further north into Scotland in an attempt to conquer the Caledonian tribes but, despite notable successes, the combination of severely stretched supply lines and a harsh landscape and climate led to a reduction in their territorial aspirations.

At the time of Hadrian's visit in 122 AD, the south of the Province flourished and prospered but the northern sector was still plagued by unrest and repeated incursions by rebel tribes. Hadrian succeeded Trajan as emperor in 117 AD; whereas his predecessor had devoted most of his reign to expanding Rome's empire with new conquests, Hadrian was more of a pragmatic consolidator. Much of his time was spent on the road; he even returned some newly conquered territories in the belief that the Empire's boundary had become too widespread and was consequently indefensible.

His assessment of the state of Britannia during that second decade of the third century led to the building of what is now known as Hadrian's Wall. He reasoned that as most of the country's natural assets were located to the south of the Tyne–Solway isthmus and only trouble lay to the north, it made perfect sense to establish a secure and defensible northern boundary to the Roman Empire. The original plans were for the western sector, between the River Irthing and Bowness, to be built from turf and the remainder in stone. In any guide to Hadrian's Wall, there are references to 'Broad' and 'Narrow' Wall. These terms relate to what was intended and what was actually built after a period of revision. Many sections of the Wall were prepared with foundations to carry the original width of 10 Roman feet (about 3 metres), but were in fact completed to a narrower width to save time and resources.

The Wall formed part of a complex military zone that not only encompassed the Wall itself, but also a forward ditch to the north and, some way back from the Wall's southern aspect, a vast earthwork known as the *vallum*. This was a deep ditch flanked on either side by high banks created from the excavated earth. Running between the Wall and the *vallum* was the military way, a minor road used to move men and materials along the Wall across more level ground. Despite ostensibly being a solid barrier, the Wall

Opposite, above: Whitley Castle, Northumberland, predates Hadrian's Wall and was a garrisoned fort, probably established to guard the Maiden Way (a Roman road over the Pennines) and the region's valuable lead mining sites.

Opposite, below: the Stanegate was marked by Roman milestones. This one at Chestersholm remains in situ, standing some 120 metres north-east of Vindolanda fort.

Right: although much of the Stanegate Roman road is now buried beneath present roads or farmland, its original course can be clearly seen on what is now the access road to the fort of Vindolanda.

was designed as a permeable structure, allowing controlled movement between north and south via designated checkpoints. As their name suggests, milecastles were placed at regular intervals and equipped with gates to allow wheeled and pedestrian traffic to pass through; they normally paid tolls for the privilege of doing so.

Each pair of milecastles was supported by two evenly spaced turrets. The system of numbering them from east to west is a twentieth-century innovation, but it does make life easier in identifying and highlighting specific sites. The turrets following each milecastle are given the same number but annotated with 'A' and 'B'. Milecastles could garrison between eight and thirty-two men and turrets could also temporarily accommodate some soldiers, but served primarily as lookout towers.

It is unlikely that much of the Wall's fabric which has survived above ground up to now dates back to its earliest second-century origins, since it was subjected to prolonged periods of repair and rebuilding under later regimes. However, in the context of both the Wall's history and that of the Roman Province of Britannia, it would be churlish to quibble over such minutiae as who rebuilt what and when it was done. It will forever be Hadrian's Wall.

~ 2 The Solway Coast

In terms of Hadrian's Wall, the Solway Firth is something of an enigma. It marks the western extremity of the Wall but, for those seeking out tangible evidence of Roman occupation, there are no piles of stones, crumbling milecastles or turrets to study along the windswept, desolate shoreline. However, the Wall was the frontier of the Roman Empire, and the northwestern tip of Cumbria is not to be disregarded simply for its apparent lack of historical sites.

Bowness-on-Solway marks the beginning of the Wall (although for those walking the recently inaugurated Hadrian's Wall Path National Trail in the recommended direction it will be the end of their trek from the River Tyne and Wallsend). Defence of the coastline continued considerably further down the Irish Sea shore, with the building of regular forts and watchtowers as far south as Maryport (Alauna) and an important naval base at Ravenglass (Itunucelum).

Viewable relics relating to that period of Irish Sea coastal fortifications are essentially restricted to just a few sites: the bath-house at Ravenglass and the clearly defined earthworks of the fort at Maryport, the latter just a few metres from the sea. Between the fort's western rampart and the beach lies the

Senhouse Roman Museum, which houses a private collection of Roman artefacts including many well-preserved altars.

The benefit of coastal fortresses has always been tempered by the simple fact that any attackers could simply sail round to the next bay and put ashore before the defending garrison had time to react. However, the Romans clearly perceived that although the Solway Firth was both fordable and navigable from the northern 'barbarian' shore, west of the fort at Bowness (Maia) the estuary is very wide. Anyone with hostile intentions would probably think twice about being forced out into the less placid waters of the open sea in what were probably not very seaworthy vessels.

Despite the obvious charms of its atmospheric coastal location and being on the start/finish line of the National Trail, Bowness-on-Solway is not really a tourist destination. There are a few more B&B signs in evidence since the official footpath opened in 2003, but so far the village seems relatively unmoved by its newly elevated status. The surroundings are perfect for nature-lovers – peat bogs, marshes and exposed mudflats make the Solway a bird watcher's paradise. Antiquarians will fare less well. Fortunately, there is still much for the casual visitor or long-distance

Opposite: sunset at low tide on the Solway Firth near Bowness-on-Solway.

walker to savour, not least the simple pleasure of just being in a place that is virtually devoid of traffic noise, where the plaintive cries of sea birds echo around a deserted shoreline and the undulating hills of Dumfries and Galloway form a creatively sculpted horizon beyond the shallow estuary.

Upon departure from Bowness, the coast road and National Trail footpath are one and the same, leaving the line of the Wall and parallel *vallum* to chart a more direct course to the next settlement, Port Carlise. Originally known as Fisher's Cross, this small coastal village was renamed during the nineteenth century when it became the entry point for an ill-fated canal that opened in 1823. The venture, intended to transport grain and other raw materials to Carlisle more reliably than was allowed by the tides and fickle estuary weather, proved financially non-viable and was abandoned just thirty years later.

Above: the Solway Firth shoreline at Bowness-on-Solway, the western extremity of Hadrian's Wall and the starting (or finishing!) point of the National Trail.

Right: at Bowness-on-Solway, a gazebo-type structure, its floor laid with Roman-style mosaic tiles, provides shelter and information for those walking the National Trail.

Above: fragmented ruins of the old port and huge blocks of red sandstone at Port Carlisle mark the site of the early nineteenth-century canal link to the centre of Carlisle.

There are still substantial remains of locks and docking quays around the shoreline, where giant red sandstone blocks bear testimony to the enterprising Victorian industrialists. Although it failed, the time, effort and money spent on the canal was not entirely wasted – it was promptly filled in when the business folded and replaced by a railway!

The next major Roman fortification on the Wall was at Drumburgh (Concavata). Excavations in the last century suggest that it was not designed as an integral part of the Wall but added later. The most substantial building in the village is Drumburgh Castle, a sixteenth-century fortified farmhouse constructed by Thomas, Lord Dacre. An earlier tower must have occupied the same site, since a licence to crenellate had been granted some two centuries previously. Although there are no inscribed stones set within the walls of the current house to serve as

Above: Drumburgh Castle is a substantial sixteenth-century fortified house, whose thick walls were largely constructed with materials from Hadrian's Wall and the nearby Roman fort.

Left: the defence of Drumburgh Castle was made significantly easier by raising the main entrance door to first-floor level.

Opposite: a retrospective view back to Drumburgh from the raised track on the fringes of the Solway Firth which roughly follows the line of the original Wall.

validation, it can be safely assumed that the builders of both structures would have benefited significantly from the adjacent Roman fort and the Wall.

The most historically significant place on the Solway stretch is Burgh-by-Sands (Aballava) which, even before the arrival of Hadrian's Wall, was the location of Roman fortifications and camps. Unfortunately, all traces of occupation from that period are lost below the modern settlement, although some sites originally situated in the immediate vicinity are more apparent in aerial surveys. Burgh was of considerable strategic importance, being located near two fording points across the Solway which were frequently used by raiding tribes from the north. The legacy of cross-border raids is manifested in the fourteenth-century fortified tower of St Michael's, a dour, squat structure that closely resembles the domestic

Above: the memorial to Edward I on the bleak expanse of Burgh Marsh, where he died in 1307. It was erected in 1803, replacing one placed there in the seventeenth century by the Duke of Norfolk.

Right: a modern statue of Edward I in the centre of Burgh-by-Sands celebrates the medieval English monarch's association with the village.

Right: St Michael's church, Burgh-by-Sands, was built from redundant stone on the site of the Roman fort of Aballava. The fourteenth-century fortified tower afforded protection to villagers during the turbulent era of cross-border raids.

pele towers which are such a distinctive architectural feature of the Scottish borders.

Despite Hadrian's influence on the region, Burgh is associated more with a much later ruler, Edward I (1239–1307), who died while encamped on the adjacent marshes prior to launching yet another of his campaigns against the Scots. A poignant memorial to the Plantagenet monarch can be found down on the marshes where he finally succumbed to dysentery. It is a worthwhile detour from the National Trail; those with cars can get closer to the site but will have to complete the last section on foot.

During the summer and early autumn, Burgh Marsh is fully exposed and comprises a vast area of rich grazing land, interlaced with tidal pools and channels. During the higher winter and spring tides, the area is frequently under water; those wishing to

Left: Beaumont church occupies the highest point of the village. Like several others along the Solway coast, it was built partially with Roman stone from the Wall; a milecastle is thought to have originally occupied the vantage point.

Opposite: the Solway marshes east of Burgh-by-Sands provide rich summer grazing for livestock.

explore the Solway Firth region should pay particular attention to local tide tables. This is such a shallow estuary that the incoming tidal waters move very fast and it is all too easy to become stranded.

On its departure from Burgh-by-Sands, Hadrian's Wall heads away from the estuary towards Carlisle, charting a course immediately south of the River Eden, one of the main rivers flowing into the Solway. The village of Beaumont occupies an elevated position overlooking one of the river's meandering loops. Hadrian's Wall ran through the centre of the current settlement, executing one of its rare, sharply angled turns in order to realign itself with the estuary's shoreline. Beaumont's name obviously comes from the Normans, the only other successful conquerors of England, who arrived a millennium later. The parish church, originally built using Wall stone, has had significant modification over time, but examples of Norman Romanesque architecture have survived over the door and around the interior's east end.

With tangible evidence of Hadrian's work being largely absent from the Solway sector, it comes as something of a relief to find a genuine Roman relic in Beaumont. It is only a solitary stone set into a wall opposite the church, but its boldly carved inscription leaves no doubt as to its provenance; its discovery is a moment to savour. Just seeing that one stone in an ordinary boundary wall emphasises the point that, from the time when people advanced from building with timber, a lump of stone was simply that and had no other value whatsoever. We should at least be thankful that whoever did build that wall in Beaumont opted to fix the stone with its inscription facing outwards.

The onward journey into Carlisle provides brief glimpses of the *vallum*, although not in any great shape or form. But, despite the absence of Roman remains, the Solway Firth is a far from wasted journey for anyone seeking to appreciate fully the scale of Hadrian's practical solution to a turbulent, unsettled and unconquerable fragment of the Empire.

Left: tangible evidence of the Roman presence in Beaumont can be clearly seen within the courses of a stone wall across the road from the church.

Overleaf: sunset at Port Carlisle.

~3 Carlisle to Birdoswald

Opposite: much of the red sandstone exterior of Carlisle Castle dates from the nineteenth century, but over 900 years of history are encased within those dour walls and ramparts.

Right: the heavily studded oak doors still guarding the main entrance to Carlisle Castle probably date to the sixteenth century.

As the first line of defence against invading forces or as strongholds from which to dominate a native population, border towns have always played a key role in the nation's history. Carlisle (Luguvalium) stands on a strategic crossing-point of the River Eden on the main western corridor between Scotland and England. It was developed as a major garrison by the Romans in the pre-Hadrianic era, when the forts of the Stanegate marked the northern border of successfully conquered Britannia. Excavation has revealed that Carlisle Castle actually stands on one corner of what was originally the site of Roman forts from the first and second centuries. During the building of the Wall, the military presence moved slightly further north to the massive, 1,000-strong cavalry garrison of Stanwyx.

Carlisle's castle has borne the brunt of many attacks and sieges during its own long history, but despite its Roman origins as a fortified site no structure within its dour, sandstone walls survives earlier than Henry I's early twelfth-century stone keep. Almost directly across the road from the castle lies the cathedral and the city's oldest surviving quarter, whose narrow cobbled streets have, sadly, been irrevocably tainted by the ubiquitous double yellow lines. This is also the location of the Tullie House Museum,

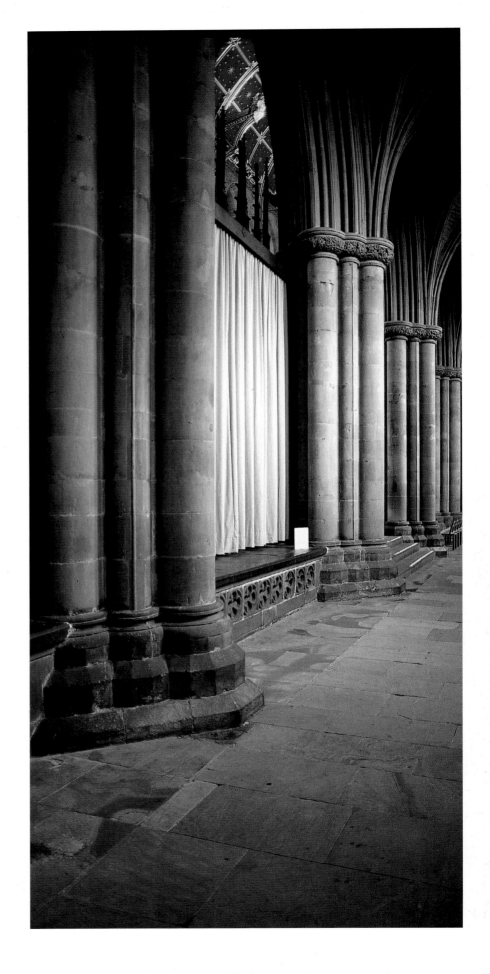

in whose gardens lie Carlisle's only Roman remains not encased in a glass cabinet – stones from a third-century shrine. It is a disappointing tally from a place of such historic significance, but it is perhaps understandable that so little has survived intact given the city's turbulent past. At least the three stones of the shrine represent a significant advance on the number encountered so far on the journey from Bowness-on-Solway!

Continuing east of Carlisle, the dearth of Roman remains persists, but the route is by no means devoid of Wall-related interest. Walkers go out of Carlisle along the course of the river as far as Crosby-on-Eden, where the path swings north to join the line of the Wall itself. Motorists may first drive to Brampton, a small market town whose first charter was granted by Henry III in 1252, before exploring two further sites with historical links to the Wall: Lanercost Priory and Bewcastle. The former requires only a minimal detour for those on foot. Visiting the latter entails an arduous fifteen-mile round trip on a bleak, moorland road, so Bewcastle may remain out of bounds to walkers on a tight schedule or with pre-booked accommodation further along the route.

Opposite, left: the scant remains of a third-century Roman shrine in the grounds of Tullie House Museum, Carlisle, are the city's sole extant link with its origins as the Stanegate fort of Luguvalium.

Opposite, right: despite being badly scarred and damaged by fire and conflict, Carlisle Cathedral retains many of its original architectural features. Where rebuilding has been necessary, old and new have been skilfully blended in almost perfect harmony.

Below: Carlisle Cathedral's origins as an Augustinian priory survive in the numerous ancillary buildings still standing within the atmospheric walled and gated precincts.

Overleaf: the River Eden near Crosby. To the east of Carlisle, the National Trail takes a route away from the barely discernible line of the Wall, opting instead for riverside walking and brief stretches along the course of the Stanegate.

Lanercost, a twelfth-century Augustinian priory, certainly benefited from the Wall's close proximity; a few inscribed stones from the Roman era are still visible in parts of its substantial surviving walls. Initially richly endowed by Robert de Vaux at its foundation in 1166, the priory frequently suffered from the bands of Scottish raiders who terrorised northern England. Ironically, the 'Hammer of the Scots' himself, Edward I, contributed to the priory's financial woes when he lodged there with a 200-strong entourage during the autumn and winter of 1306. What had originally been scheduled as a short halt en route to Carlisle and Scotland became a protracted stay when the king was taken ill. He remained until the following March, which must have placed an almost unbearable strain on the priory's resources. He made little progress afterwards, either towards Scotland or the end of his fourth decade on the throne; he died just a few months later on Burgh Marsh.

Above: Lanercost bridge dates from the eighteenth century and carried traffic over the River Irthing until 1962.

Right: Brampton's early nineteenth-century Moot Hall. The Cumbrian market town, granted a charter by Henry III in 1252, is 3 kilometres south of the Wall and its old parish church was built using Wall stone.

Opposite: Lanercost Priory was less than 800 metres south of the Wall, providing its builders with an easy source of material.

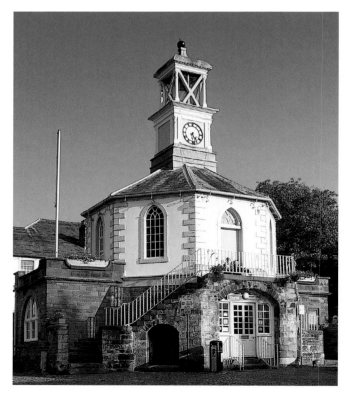

Bewcastle is an extraordinarily beguiling place, lying isolated in barren countryside midway between Hadrian's Wall and the Scottish border. It comprises just a couple of dwellings: the small parish church and the gaunt remains of a medieval castle that was built on the north-east corner of a Hadrianic-period fort. It was one of several substantial Roman outposts established beyond the Empire's northern wall and was linked by a direct road to the major Wall fort at Birdoswald. However, notwithstanding its important military associations, Bewcastle is really renowned for the magnificent late seventh- or early eighth-century Anglo-Saxon cross in St Cuthbert's church-yard. Sadly, the top is lost but the surviving base of the cross, 4.5 metres high, is arguably the finest of the few examples in England that have survived the intervening twelve centuries.

The cross is richly carved with interlaced knot work, runic inscriptions and three figures: John the

Above: the Norman castle at Bewcastle was one of three northern outpost forts built around the same time as the Wall.

Right: the vibrant carvings and inscriptions on the Bewcastle Cross may be succumbing to the effects of harsh Border weather and rapacious lichen, but this remains one of England's most evocative early Christian sites.

Above: from Banks East Turret's elevated position there are wide-ranging views to the south across the valley of the River Irthing.

Above right: Pike Hill Signal Tower predates Hadrian's Wall, having been built as part of the Stanegate's defence network. Although later incorporated into the Wall, the tower's original orientation meant that it remained sited at an oblique angle.

Baptist, Christ, and one other that some experts have interpreted as being St John the Evangelist. Not only is the cross itself a magnificent monument in its own right, but its erection in such a remote location is equally remarkable, attesting to an early Christian presence on a site probably first occupied by a Roman temple attached to the original fort. Bewcastle's Roman name, Fanuum Cocidii, means Temple of Cocidus, a Germanic war god, so there would not appear to have been much common ground between the beliefs of the legionaries and Northumberland's pre-Conquest Christian population. Yet it is conceivable that those responsible for the cross saw the continuity of religious worship in the same place as beneficial, despite the pagan nature of those who preceded them.

On retracing one's steps from Bewcastle back to where the line of Hadrian's Wall passes through the small village of Banks, those travelling from the Solway are finally rewarded with the first substantial Roman remains: Banks East Turret and Pike Hill Signal Tower. The road at this point is very narrow but an adjacent lay-by offers parking and an opportunity to explore both sites in safety; a gravel footpath connects the turret to the higher signal tower. For walkers who have opted to travel east–west along the National Trail, Banks East Turret marks the last real contact with the Wall and the remaining 50 kilometres or so must be something of an anti-climax. However, the reverse applies to those journeying towards the rising sun: the sight of Hadrian's Wall carving its way across the dramatic escarpment of the Whin Sill is an experience yet to be savoured.

Although later rebuilt in stone, this section of the Wall – from its crossing of the River Irthing at Willowford (see Chapter 4) to the Solway – was initially built of turf. This strategy was probably employed to ensure the speediest possible completion of the barrier, there being no sources of easily quarried and transportable building stone readily available west of the Whin Sill region. A programme of consolidation in stone was undertaken later, replacing not only the Wall, but also the milecastles which had also been constructed from turf and timber. An indication of what the original turf wall may have looked like can be seen to the south, midway between Pike Hill and Birdoswald. In most places, the stone wall directly replaced its turf counterpart, but in the vicinity of High House Farm and also to the east of Birdoswald Fort it charted a slightly realigned course.

Closer to Birdoswald, the smaller intermediate turrets required no upgrading: they had all been built

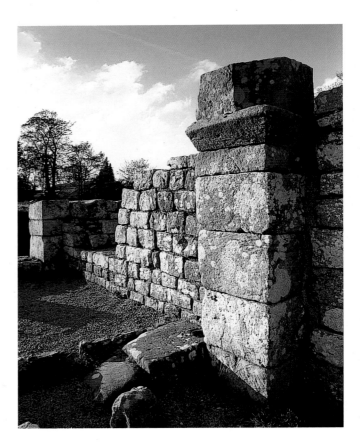

Left: the Birdoswald site has experienced continuous post-Roman occupation, evolving from an Anglo-Saxon timber dwelling through to the fortified tower house and farm which now form the English Heritage Visitor Centre and Museum.

Right: the east gate of Birdoswald is one of the most complete examples of such a structure within any of the Wall forts. The jamb of the north portal stands to an impressive height.

of stone from the outset and a couple of examples, Piper Sike and Leahill, lie by the roadside between Pike Hill and Birdoswald Fort. Pike Hill, commanding a wide panorama, was perfectly sited to fulfil its role as a signalling station, although it was commissioned much earlier than Hadrian's Wall and formed part of the Stanegate's defensive network.

A substantial stretch of Wall running directly alongside the modern road provides a fitting prelude to one's arrival at the fort of Birdoswald (Banna), whose north-eastern corner is now dominated by an imposing cluster of buildings, including a nine-teenth-century replica of an earlier pele, or tower house, which occupied the same site. The fort's location was strategically well chosen, since beyond its southern boundary a near-precipitous bank drops down into a gorge created by the River Irthing. The fort, originally built to straddle the turf wall that runs to the south of its later stone replacement, was probably also made of turf and timber; it was later relocated to its current alignment with the Wall. It housed a cavalry unit during its earlier 'turf wall' years, but subsequently became an infantry base.

Opposite: the ruined exterior defensive wall of Birdoswald still conveys the sense of power and military might associated with the Roman occupation.

Overleaf: sunset on Hadrian's Wall above Walltown Crags.

Records show that for a substantial period it was home to the 1,000-strong First Aelian Cohort of Dacians, a regiment originating in the Roman Province of Dacia on the Lower Danube in what is now Romania.

Impressive granaries have been exposed near the modern buildings but major excavations have not yet been undertaken; until fairly recently the site was a working farm and much of the fort's interior has been left undisturbed. As a consequence, the vast grassy area encompassed within the perimeter walls gives one a good impression of the size and scale of a typical Roman fort. The extant walls are of moderate height, but the east gate stands out as the finest example of a monumental gate anywhere along the Wall. Birdoswald has already yielded much to archaeologists and historians, who have benefited from recent advances in science and computer technology. However, in the fullness of time, the tried and trusted method of spade, trowel and fine-haired brushes will undoubtedly be employed to reveal even more treasures lying beneath the hitherto undisturbed earth.

$\sim$ 4 Birdoswald to Cawfields

Opposite: the first section of the Wall heading east from Birdoswald towards Milecastle 49 is of impressive height and thickness. It is also renowned for the inscriptions on some of the stones.

Below: the sculpted phallus is more of a protective talisman than any statement about the creator's virility!

From the exit gate of Birdoswald Fort's excellent English Heritage Visitor Centre, an unbroken length of Wall runs across a grazed pasture towards Harrow's Scar and Milecastle 49. From the Solway Firth as far as that milecastle the original turf structure was replaced by stone, using 'Narrow' Wall specifications (about 2 metres wide), with matching foundations. This contrasts with the technique employed further east, where many sections of foundations had already been laid for a 'Broad' Wall (about 3 metres wide), prior to the plans being amended and a 'Narrow' Wall built upon the wider footings.

The Wall near Birdoswald is noted for possessing a number of stones bearing 'building inscriptions', carved to mark which Legion was responsible for completing a particular segment. The discoloration of the stones over time has made these more difficult to spot, but playing 'hunt the graffiti' might amuse bored children, especially if they manage to find that perfectly accepted device for inducing luck and warding off evil, the carved phallus!

At this point of eastward progression along the Wall, the wave-like undulations of the Whin Sill appear more prominently on the horizon. That irregular terrain presented its own set of problems to the

Above: the Wall to the east of Willowford climbs steeply away from the meandering River Irthing and, en route to Gilsland, exhibits how the revised 'Narrow' Wall was built upon the original broad foundations.

Above right: despite being fashioned from metal, the current footbridge over the Irthing at Willowford is not only aesthetically pleasing but cleverly designed to connect both sides of a river whose banks are at radically different heights.

builders, though a more immediate natural obstacle to overcome was the River Irthing. Milecastle 49 is perched on the edge of Harrow's Scar, a steep escarpment overlooking the winding river some distance below. The stone milecastle was built over its turf predecessor, and from this point the two diverged, following different routes until well past Birdoswald.

Although the top of Harrow's Scar is thick with trees and vegetation, it is possible to get an aerial view of the Wall as it temporarily terminates at the Willowford Bridge abutment. The eastern base of the Roman bridge is now marooned in the middle of a field, the erosive power of the river having taken it upon a more westerly course since it was bridged by the Legion's engineers. From the scant walls of the milecastle, a path winds down to the river and a modern footbridge, a prefabricated iron structure that was lowered into place from a helicopter in a complex

and highly skilled operation. On closer inspection, the ruins of the second-century bridge works still bear traces of drainage channels or sluice gates. Arguably of greater interest is the retrospective view to the dark face of Harrow's Scar. It is a forbidding prospect, leaving one to speculate on just how the project would have been accomplished had the river run beneath that sheer face of earth and rock. The Wall climbs quite sharply upwards from the valley floor, passing immediately next to Willowford Farm before levelling out and running on towards Gilsland.

The difference in the width of the Wall and its foundations can be clearly discerned at this point and also at Willowford East Turret (48A), whose protruding wings were clearly designed and built to accept the 'Broad' Wall. The Wall continues for another 100 metres and is then swallowed up by the last few houses on the outskirts of Gilsland. National

Right: Milecastle 49, also
known as Harrow's Scar,
occupies a commanding
viewpoint above the near-
precipitous sides of the
Irthing valley.

Left: Turret 48A at Gilsland is still high enough to provide a modicum of shelter to walkers on the National Trail. It was originally built to be part of the 'Broad' Wall but was left with protruding 'wings' when the narrow revision was pursued.

Trail walkers are directed across the road and on to a footpath that leads to Poltross Burn Milecastle (48), one of the Wall's better-preserved examples. That it has survived at all is a miracle, standing as it does within a couple of metres of a busy railway line and the viaduct carrying it over the stream after which the milecastle is named.

Motorists have a choice of two access points; both involve some walking and carry a degree of risk. Those who park near the Wall and follow the route taken by the Trail walkers will experience the frisson of terror and uncertainty associated with safely negotiating an unmarked rail crossing; the tracks may be straight but trains do seem to arrive disconcertingly quickly after an initial sighting. The other option is to drive to the other end of Gilsland and park near the viaduct, but that walk involves climbing a very steep flight of steps to access the milecastle. Regardless of how one does arrive, the rewards are well

Above: Milecastle 48 (Poltross Burn) stands next to the railway that runs over the line of the Wall. Fortuitously, the engineering works did not destroy the milecastle, although it does rattle a bit when heavy quarry trains rumble past!

Left: Milecastle 48 contains the unique feature of a flight of three steps which led up to the building's wall walk.

worth the effort – the ruins are not particularly high, but are most informative.

Poltross Burn Milecastle appears larger than many of its contemporaries, having two generously sized barrack blocks and traces of ovens in one corner. Its most arresting feature, and the subject of much conjecture, is a flight of three steps inside the north-eastern wall which would have led up to a parapet or walkway. By hypothetically projecting the steps upwards, experts have deduced that the height of the building was probably in the region of 4 metres, but there are imponderables. Did the steps lead to a walkway that was itself protected by a higher parapet? Did legionaries use a rudimentary stepladder to gain extra height from the top of the steps? Oh, the glorious uncertainties of history!

Car drivers may pursue the option of visiting the stark remains of Thirlwall Castle; walkers will automatically encounter the fourteenth-century fortress

because it lies directly on the National Trail path. The real excitement is but a *ballista* (catapult) bolt's flight away at Walltown Crags: the place where Hadrian's Wall begins its switchback ride over the Whin Sill ridge. The Whin Sill is thought to derive its name from North Pennine dialects in which 'whin' means hard and 'sill', more obviously, a flat bed of rock. The rock in question is an ancient quartz dolorite that forced its way up through beds of softer sandstone and limestone during bouts of geological upheaval in the Carboniferous period, over 280 million years ago. The Whin Sill is characterised by a rugged, sheer, northern face that mellows into a gentler southern slope, a combination that perfectly suited the Roman surveyors who worked so effectively in conjunction with nature to create their defensive barrier.

The very rock endowing the landscape of Hadrian's Wall with its unique character was also, curiously, nearly the catalyst for its downfall. Because of its hardness and durability, whinstone was highly prized for road-building in the first half of the twentieth century; quarries at locations such as Cawfields and Walltown Crags showed scant regard for the nation's priceless heritage. The latter is now in an advanced stage of restoration, the vast quarry being converted from a debris-filled industrial site to a National Park recreation area. One can clearly see the Wall perched high above the face of the quarried crags; without government intervention in the early 1940s, considerably more might have been blasted away.

Access to the top of Walltown Crags could not be easier, courtesy of two conveniently sited car parks

Above: Thirlwall Castle was constructed during the early fourteenth century, using recycled Roman stone. Although located a short distance from the line of the Wall, the castle lies directly on the route of the National Trail.

Opposite: at Walltown Crags, Hadrian's Wall ends abruptly at an artificial escarpment, created by the stone quarry that had already consumed stretches of the Wall in its path.

Opposite: Turret 45A and the view east beyond Walltown Crags.

Right: the scant remains of Great Chesters fort (Aesica) are located near an isolated farm west of Cawfields.

Far right: the altar at Great Chesters fort seems to have been adopted by visitors as a form of 'wishing well': the shallow indentation carved on its top to receive offerings is now full of copper coins.

and a network of well-surfaced footpaths. Apart from the Wall itself, the main architectural feature above Walltown Crags is Turret 45A, particularly noteworthy since it was already in existence when the Wall was being constructed. This can be clearly seen as it is not in perfect alignment with the Wall; it is also devoid of the wing walls normally associated with similar structures. One can readily see why the turret was placed in that location, since the view is an almost unbroken 360-degree panorama. Walking along the summit of Walltown Crags also gives a first-hand glimpse of how difficult the terrain must have been for the builders to follow. Almost without warning, what seems to be a sustained stretch of turf suddenly nosedives into a rocky dip before rising up sharply again to repeat the process a little further on.

The elevated Walltown ridge gradually moderates as it progresses east, descending and levelling out on to a network of fields, in one of which lie the fragmentary ruins of Great Chesters Fort (Aesica). Despite its forlorn appearance, I found this small fort one of the most endearing places along the Wall; its crumbling, bleached and partially overgrown masonry somehow endows the site with a greater sense of history than the more fully excavated examples which now sit primly in areas of neatly mown grass. Great Chesters has not been ignored by archaeologists; several excavations over an extended period, not least one at the end of the nineteenth century, resulted in the discovery of several important items of jewellery. The treasure included a hare-shaped enamelled brooch and a gilded bronze Celtic brooch. More recent specialised aerial photography, using

Left: the sharp edge of Cawfields Crags in profile, revealing just how close quarrying came to engulfing and destroying Milecastle 42. The site has now been landscaped and provides easy access to the Wall and the impressive remains of the milecastle.

Overleaf: Milecastle 42, Cawfields Crags.

infra-red film, has revealed the configuration of the fort in greater detail, how its defensive ditches were aligned around the perimeter and also the extent and precise location of the civilian settlement (*vicus*). Great Chesters is accessible only to pedestrians; even walking from the nearest car park at Cawfields is a round trip of 2.5 kilometres.

Motorists seeking to 'cherry pick' the Wall's high-lights will certainly include Cawfields Crags on their itinerary. When first seen from the access road, the combination of Hadrian's Wall, Milecastle 42 and the sawn-off crag present an extraordinary spectacle. Cawfields was another of the Wall's infamous whinstone quarries, continuing in operation until 1952, but it appears at first glance to have been less destructive than its more westerly neighbour. Having said that, the quarrying came uncomfortably close to gobbling up the dramatically located milecastle, as can be seen when the Crag is viewed in profile. Both that site and an exhilarating stretch of Wall are readily accessible from the quarry's car park, via a path running alongside the old flooded workings.

$\sim$5 Cawfields to Housesteads

Because the old stone quarry at Cawfields Crags is more compact than the Walltown site, the perception might be that it perhaps inflicted less damage to Hadrian's Wall than its larger neighbour. As one walks alongside the artificial lake towards the squat, triangular crag face the scene looks innocuous enough, but after passing through the two kissing gates giving access to the crag's eastern flank and Milecastle 42, the true scale of past industrial vandalism becomes immediately apparent. The Wall soars up the severely truncated undulation of the Whin Sill and simply stops, sliced off and reduced to rubble by those who placed a higher value upon road stone than Roman stones.

Fortunately, the work stopped just in time to save Milecastle 42 which, despite being devoid of any surviving traces of internal buildings, presents an impressive sight; doubly so if one scrambles up to the apex of the adjacent savaged crag. With that height advantage, a panorama of bleak, desolate countryside opens up beyond the Wall and its milecastle, a tableau conveying a sense of how utterly dreary life on the frontier must have been. It speaks volumes for the discipline and sense of purpose that must have prevailed within the Roman Legions and many auxiliary units garrisoned along the Wall.

The milecastle was built on a quite severe south-facing slope, which must have made both the construction and occupation more than a little difficult. Excavation has revealed that its north gate was built using significantly larger than normal blocks of masonry, probably in support of a tower. However, it does seem extraordinary that a controlled gateway and road should have run through the centre of such an inaccessible building when the pass it controlled, Hole Gap, was such a short distance to the west.

The long, gradual ascent from Milecastle 42 towards Thorny Doors, the next natural gap in the crags, is alongside a particularly fine section of restored Wall with wide-ranging views. Although frequently lost to farming activity or simply degraded by age, the *vallum* is a prominent feature immediately to the south of Cawfields Crags, its ditch and flanking earth mounds clearly etched on the landscape. Having overcome the chasm of Thorny Doors, the Wall makes its way to Caw Gap and another of the conveniently placed minor roads providing motorists with easier access to different sections. In the vicinity of Caw Gap, the Wall has not survived to any great height, but this is more than compensated for by the sight of it snaking up the hillside on the eastern side of the pass towards Winshields Crags.

Opposite: the Wall begins its dramatic descent to Thorny Doors, one of several natural breaches in the crags of the Whin Sill.

In the midst of a timeless landscape and a 2,000-year-old stone wall, the white concrete trig point on the summit of Winshields Crags is visually disruptive. However, it marks the highest point of Hadrian's Wall so, however mundane, it becomes a landmark in its own right. It is surprising and rather disappointing to discover that despite the Whin Sill's physical stature it cannot muster a summit of more than 345 metres. It might be better to go along with the fell-walker Alfred Wainwright's insistence that British mountains should retain their imperial measurements – this policy would elevate the summit to a more impressive-sounding 1,132 feet above sea level!

Winshields may be the highest point attained by Hadrian's Wall, but the fabric of the Wall itself and the overall views are more impressive elsewhere. Peel Gap and Steel Rigg are the next particularly noteworthy locations. A gentle amble east from the trig point leads to a formal car park run by the National Park Authority, a popular destination for day-visitors. The almost sheer face of Peel Crags lies south-west of the car park, and a steep, winding set of stone steps leads walkers up on to the plateau of Steel Rigg. For anyone preferring not to attempt that sharp ascent, an alternative path skirts to the south of the crags, tracing the route of the old Military Way.

Opposite: a view north-west across the undulating farmland that lies beyond the Wall near Caw Gap.

Above left: the trig point on Winshields Crags which marks the highest elevation attained by Hadrian's Wall.

Above right: from the precipitous edge of the crags leading down to Peel Gap, there is a perfect view down to the turret that was a strategic afterthought, being inserted between the established turrets 39A and 39B.

The retrospective view from the top of Peel Crags reveals a curious anomaly immediately below: the outline of an additional turret erected to control the wide access point of Peel Gap. Despite the Romans' normal adherence to precise spacing between turrets and milecastles, even they were forced to acknowledge that there was a defensive loophole at this location, and they obviously took remedial action. The most surprising thing about the Peel Gap turret is that it was not discovered and excavated until 1986 – but then why would anybody go hunting for something that, in theory, should not have existed?

From Steel Rigg right through to Housesteads, Hadrian's Wall is at its visually dramatic best, soaring and dipping over several severe undulations on the Whin Sill escarpment. The first section is one of the best examples of the nineteenth-century 'Clayton' Wall (see Chapter 6); although it has been rebuilt to a uniform width and height, the symmetry adds to rather than detracts from the aura of power and achievement that surrounds Hadrian's Wall. Each of the extant milecastles has its own individual qualities of architectural merit or setting within the landscape; Milecastle 39 (also known as Castle Nick) has the additional element of glorious surprise. As one walks along the comparatively level heights of Steel

Rigg, the ground suddenly falls away into a deep hollow and there, at its base, lies the familiar 'playing card' outline of the milecastle. Castle Nick retains traces of its internal layout: the barracks and other buildings occupied by the soldiers during their tour of duty in that isolated mini-garrison. Given that the milecastle's longest wall is only about 19 metres, living conditions must have been fairly cramped.

Almost immediately after climbing up and away from Castle Nick, an even steeper descent leads down into Sycamore Gap. The mature tree that has given the narrow cleft its name could not have been better placed, even if deliberately planted there, the elegant shape of its branches combining with the steep-sided bowl to create a scene of almost perfect natural harmony. Sycamore Gap is not only aesthetically pleasing; in terms of the Wall's history, it has proved to be one of the more informative sites investigated by archaeologists.

Builders are renowned for leaving debris lying around a site and it seems that the Romans were no different. Their late second-century rubbish has yielded important information about the Wall after the Hadrianic era. Pottery and other datable materials from that period of repair and restoration work were discovered within the Wall at Sycamore Gap.

Above: a detail of the Wall on Steel Rigg, showing the difficulty of the task faced by Roman masons in coping with the terrain's constant undulations.

Opposite: the impressive remains of Milecastle 39, also known as Castle Nick, lie sheltered in a hollow of the Whin Sill, perfectly encapsulating the astounding achievement of its second-century builders.

Below: a retrospective view westwards past the deep cleft of Sycamore Gap.

Right: Sycamore Gap is one of the Wall's best-known features, elegantly occupied by the mature tree that must be one of the most photographed specimens in Northumberland!

These finds confirm the belief that having been de-commissioned and neglected in favour of the ill-fated Antonine Wall in Scotland (built on the orders of Hadrian's successor, Antonious Pius, r. 138–161) Hadrian's original fortified border was reinstated as the most northerly part of the Roman Empire.

Walkers will have been catching occasional glimpses of Crag Lough's shimmering waters during their eastbound progression from the heights of Winshields. After the ascent from Sycamore Gap the lake becomes a more prominent feature, running parallel to the Wall at the foot of Highshields Crags' severe cliffs. The lake is one of several in the region formed by glacial action during the last Ice Age, when a glacier scooped a depression out of layers of softer rock and the resulting shallow bowl filled with water.

During the latter stages of the walk above Crag Lough, the Wall enters a band of trees before emerging near the lake's eastern shore at a break in the Whin Sill called Milking Gap. The name, thought to have originated in the eighteenth century, refers to the shelters that were erected to afford protection to those milking the cattle that grazed on the neighbouring upland pastures. This important pass through the Whin Sill bears faint, but tangible, evidence of a native tribal settlement in the form of circular dwellings encompassed within a rectangular enclosure.

The track through Milking Gap leads up past Hotbank Farm and the Wall is rejoined, climbing once again to begin the most dramatic section along its entire length. After a brief level part, the first of several steep gullies is encountered as the Wall

Above: Crag Lough and Highshields Crags.

Opposite: the Wall plunges down to Rapishaw Gap, a natural break in the crags, where the Pennine Way long-distance footpath forges north towards the Cheviots and the Scottish border.

Above: the Wall on its descent to Rapishaw Gap.

Left: the National Trail footpath sign, directing Pennine Way walkers away from the Wall and onwards to their journey's end in Scotland.

Opposite: the Wall pauses briefly at Rapishaw Gap and the rugged western end of Cuddy's Crags.

descends into Rapishaw Gap. This marks the place where those on the Pennine Way long-distance footpath are diverted through the Wall and onwards up to Northumberland's vast tracts of conifer plantations, the Cheviot and their journey's end at Kirk Yetholm in the Scottish Borders. One fervently hopes that few will cross the ladder-stile without first making an essential detour to Milecastle 37 and Housesteads Fort. The former lies at the bottom of one of several severe undulations en route to the fort itself; for those whose leg muscles are starting to protest, the Military Way offers a more direct and benign method of reaching Housesteads. However, this is a route only for those on the verge of collapse, since to pursue it is to miss out on the very essence of the Wall.

Milecastle 37 lies little more than a quarter of a mile from Housesteads Fort and is noted for the monumental masonry of its north gate, comprising giant blocks of stone rising up to the springers of the arch. However, this impressive sight is more to do with modern excavation and restoration than the skills of those who originally built the milecastle; archaeologists have deduced that it collapsed shortly after completion due to inadequate foundations, and was never reinstated. After a final climb from Milecastle 37, the path runs along the top of the Wall as it

passes through a copse of trees before emerging at the fort's north-western corner.

Housesteads Fort (Vercovicium) is undoubtedly the 'flagship' site of Hadrian's Wall, superbly managed and presented by English Heritage on behalf of the National Trust. For those walking along the Wall the hard work has already been completed, but motorists will have to leave their cars in the Information Centre car park alongside the B6318 and walk the final few hundred metres. It is a deceptively stiff climb up to the fort and adjacent museum, but those who make the effort will be well rewarded. The fort is still surrounded by its curtain wall, encompassing a five-acre site that housed a cohort of around 800 men. From the early nineteenth century through to the 1980s, Housesteads has been comprehensively excavated to reveal the substantial remains of several internal buildings. The sense of history pervading the site is doubly increased by the fact that Hadrian's Wall remains in situ and is incorporated into the fort's north-facing perimeter. The Wall briefly disappears from view as it dips down towards the Knag Burn before soaring up over Sewingshields Crags, the final leg of its spectacular journey across the Whin Sill.

Above: the view east towards Housesteads from Cuddy's Crags.

Above: Milecastle 37, near Housesteads Fort.

Right: the partially restored north gate of Milecastle 37 is one of the most impressive architectural features along the entire length of the Wall.

70

Opposite, above: the north gate of Housesteads Fort, looking north-east towards Sewingshields Crags.

Opposite: the commander's house (praetorium) was the largest building within the fort.

Above: the granaries are one of the more impressive and informative surviving features of Housesteads Fort. The stone pillars supported a raised floor to eliminate damp and ensure that food remained free from vermin.

Overleaf: a view to the south-west over the snow-clad ruins of Housesteads Fort.

ᨠ6 Archaeology & Living History

It was not until the mid-nineteenth century that Hadrian's Wall was transformed from being a source of ready-dressed building stone or a mere object of curiosity into a priceless historical resource, to be investigated, excavated and subsequently protected. A handful of intrepid travellers and historians made their way up to the Wall during the late sixteenth and seventeenth centuries, most notably William Camden (1551–1623), who journeyed extensively throughout the British Isles collecting material for his monumental chorography, *Britannia*. However, the border country of Northumberland was hardly the safest of places to be wandering around clutching a notebook and sketchpad, so it was not until the era of widespread and more secure travel in the eighteenth century that people's personal horizons were broadened. Some members of the social elite who had crossed the Channel and the Alps on the Grand Tour returned home inspired by the architecture of Ancient Rome, and formed antiquarian societies to further their quest for knowledge. Others just came home and dreamed of Empire building!

Notable eighteenth-century antiquaries such as the Rev. John Horsley and William Stukeley conducted detailed research into the history and origins of the Wall, but it was not until the following century that archaeological excavation got under way in earnest. One man in particular, John Clayton (1792–1890), is justifiably lauded as the saviour of Hadrian's Wall. Such a claim may seem extravagant, but without his tireless and altruistic endeavour, the principle sites and most dramatic sections of the Wall that we take for granted today might simply not have survived.

During the 1830s, Clayton, head of his family's law firm, was appointed Town Clerk of Newcastle upon Tyne, a post he occupied to good effect: he was responsible for considerable development within the city. As the wealthy owner of the Chesters estate (which, coincidentally, happened to have a Hadrianic cavalry fort buried within its parkland), he was able to devote his spare time and considerable resources in pursuit of his private passion: uncovering the secrets of the Roman wall. Chesters was relatively close to the wilder sections of the Wall, so he spent many hours walking amid the crags and ridges of the Whin Sill that carried the remains of the Roman frontier. He was appalled at the way landowners persistently plundered its stone, showing scant regard for the Wall's historic value.

No conservation bodies such as the National Trust, English Heritage or the National Parks Authority

Opposite: 'Roman legionaries' marching in formation at an English Heritage re-enactment event.

existed at that time, and the concept of 'heritage' was restricted to an enlightened minority. Anyone who happened to have a ruined ancient monument on their land was entitled to treat it as just another resource, rather than as something to be revered. Clayton resolved to take practical measures to address this problem. From 1834, he began buying farms and other properties within the Roman military zone whenever they came up for sale. His labourers were then tasked with the job of clearing and rebuilding long sections of the Wall on his newly acquired property. The 'Clayton' Wall is clearly distinguishable from other sections. It is uniform in appearance, having being rebuilt generally to a height of seven courses and sealed with a turf capping rather than mortared stones. This technique contrasts with that employed in the twentieth century on other sections of the Wall in which no recreation of the original took place, whatever remained in situ being secured by the use of modern, weatherproof cements. Sections of the Wall treated in the newer manner are now referred to as 'Consolidated' Wall.

In addition to restoring long sections of Hadrian's Wall over the Whin Sill, Clayton also began a programme of excavation on the various milecastles, turrets and forts encompassed within his expanding

estate. His most extensive and best-known research was, unsurprisingly, carried out in his own back garden. In addition to a substantial number of original buildings, the cavalry fort of Cilernum at Chesters yielded a rich harvest of altars, tombstones and other artefacts, many of which are displayed in the wonderful on-site museum. The Clayton Collection is housed in a Victorian building untainted by modern technology. No computer graphics or simulations guide visitors through hi-tech representations of the past: the rows of neatly labelled exhibits are simply displayed and allowed to speak for themselves in an almost reverential silence.

Pioneering archaeologists in Clayton's wake made even further progress towards discovering more about the lives of those who built, lived and served along the Roman frontier, and advances in modern science and excavation techniques have moved that process further forward in leaps and bounds. The Stanegate fort of Vindolanda has long been the focus of intensive investigation in a programme of research ongoing to this day. One can never confidently predict the future, but it seems unlikely that any new discoveries will have greater significance than the Vindolanda Writing Tablets, the first batch of which were found in 1973.

Opposite, left: the section of Hadrian's Wall running over Peel Crags is a fine example of nineteenth-century restoration by John Clayton. Original facing stones were re-laid without recourse to mortar, secured, then sealed with turf.

Opposite, right: a geometric riverbank 'rockery' has been fashioned with stones from the adjacent Chesters Bridge abutment on the east bank of the North Tyne.

Above and right: John Clayton made a remarkable collection of altar stones and other artefacts amassed during his excavation of Chesters and other forts (Chesters Museum).

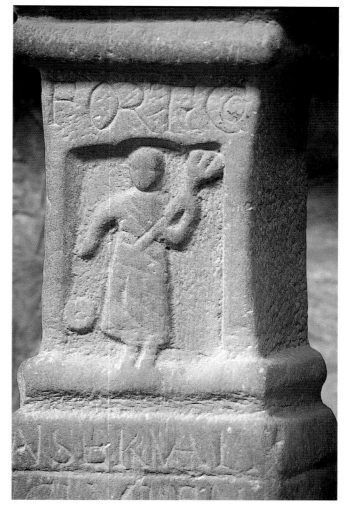

Left: an interior view of one of the sparsely furnished barrack buildings at Arbeia. When combined with the activities of Roman military re-enactment groups, such reconstructions create an engaging educational resource.

Below: twin pillars still stand in what was the courtyard of the headquarters building of Arbeia. One of the reconstructed barrack blocks is in the background.

Because the fort pre-dated the Wall, its earlier timber versions saw several periods of rebuilding and replacement prior to a final reconstruction in stone. It was customary practice to establish a clean, firm base on which to erect a new fort by sealing the existing site with a solid layer of clay and turf, a process that created an almost sterile, anaerobic environment. What is thought to have been one of those earlier garrison's rubbish tips was found, containing a large quantity of wood tablets of varying sizes, many about the size of a small notebook. And that is indeed what they were, bearing letters to families and loved ones back home in the Roman provinces of mainland Europe, along with lists of supplies and other documents relating to the fort's daily administration.

That they survived at all is remarkable, but it is even more astonishing that the ink writing was still decipherable. Judging by some of the contents, they could have been written or received by any serving soldier from the second century to the present day — the grumbles, hopes and fears of men on the front line and their loved ones back home are always the same! The Tablets, now displayed in the British Museum, are essential viewing for anyone seeking to glean more in-depth knowledge about the period of Roman occupation.

One of the more remarkable stories concerning the history of archaeological research along the Wall relates to the fort of Arbeia at South Shields. Located several miles east of Wallsend on the south bank of the River Tyne's mouth, it performed an important role as a supply base, particularly during the post-Hadrianic era when the Antonine Wall was established. During the first phases of archaeological exploration in the nineteenth century most sites were obviously in private ownership, but in 1875 the South Shields fort became the first to be taken into the care of a local government authority. The greenfield site had been on the verge of development when Roman remains were unearthed. This led to further excavation and the eventual creation by the Council of the wonderfully named People's Roman Remains Park.

The site is still being investigated. It is most remarkable for the various reconstructed buildings which faithfully recreate the originals, helping to make Arbeia an invaluable educational resource. Visitors can see how soldiers lived in cramped barrack blocks and savour the more refined surroundings of the Courtyard House, probably home to the Commanding Officer and his family. Reconstructions and accurate props bring the past vividly to life, especially when live actors form part of the recreation.

Right: the reconstructed west gate of Arbeia, the Roman fort built on the mouth of the River Tyne at South Shields.

Far left: whenever possible, food is prepared using the original methods and recipes unearthed in historical documents and other reference sources.

Left: cooking over open fires, with meat such as lamb wrapped in vine leaves.

Far left: charcoal, used with earthenware vessels, provided a controllable heat source, in the same way that today's cook uses a regulated oven.

Left: a collection of finished dishes at a Roman cookery demonstration, including bread, a form of pesto and stuffed kidneys.

'Living History' events are now a regular feature at such sites, especially those in the care of English Heritage such as Chesters and Corbridge. The staged events may contain a high entertainment factor, but behind the colour and pageantry lies a wealth of research and attention to historical detail. Those who belong to historical re-enactment groups take their roles very seriously, ensuring that all costumes, armour and weaponry are made as accurately as possible by thoroughly researching historical documents and noting representations of people and artefacts in ancient Roman sculpture.

Set-piece military activities in fenced-off arenas display army tactics and battle drill, but the fringe demonstrations can be of even greater interest.

Craftsmen, jewellers and metalworkers beaver away at tables and mini-forges to produce wares using techniques and raw materials as close as possible to those of their Roman forebears. Cookery is an integral part of any such day; again, only authentic methods of food preparation and cooking are used, although not all the raw ingredients can be guaranteed to be exactly those used to feed hungry legionaries!

Many members of these groups actively contribute to educational programmes in schools. There is really no comparison between the amount of attention a history textbook is likely to get from a bored pupil and the stories of a fully armoured 'Roman centurion'.

Below: re-enactment groups exhibit real skills, such as those that would have been practised by specialist craftsmen within a legion. Here, sandals are being made in the Roman style.

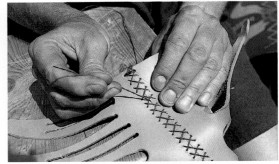

Below: the Cornicen (horn blower) was a vital link in the command chain, using the instrument to issue commands in much the same way that the bugle was used in more recent times.

Right: re-enactment groups undertake meticulous research to ensure that their armour and clothing is an accurate representation of that originally worn by their second-century peers.

Below right: the Roman army used several heavier weapons including the ballista, essentially a giant, high-powered crossbow. Even though it was a functional piece of field artillery, many were elaborately decorated, as here, with the legion's insignia.

Above: a statue depicting the birth of Mithras, recovered from the Mithraeum at Housesteads, is now an important element of a reconstructed Mithraic temple. The powerfully symbolic sculpture depicts Mithras emerging from the egg of the Cosmos, bearing the Sword of Truth and the Torch of Light; the egg's rim is decorated with the twelve signs of the Zodiac. (Museum of Antiquities, Newcastle upon Tyne.)

Above: an altar to the sea gods Neptune and Oceanus dedicated in 122 AD by the Sixth Legion, responsible for constructing the first bridge over the Tyne in Newcastle, the Pons Aelius. A large fish is entwined around Neptune's distinctive trident – it seems entirely appropriate that this altar was recovered from the river. (Museum of Antiquities, Newcastle upon Tyne.)

Above: this well-preserved altar was discovered during excavations at Corbridge; it is one of the many exhibits housed in the on-site English Heritage museum. The Roman fort and town has been the subject of several major twentieth-century excavations, one of the most notable being that conducted between 1906 and 1914 by Francis Haverfield (1860–1919), Camden Professor of Ancient History at the University of Oxford.

Above: a third-century relief portraying Venus bathing at a spring with attendant nymphs. It was recovered from the outpost fort of High Rochester and probably once adorned a sacred spring (Museum of Antiquities, Newcastle upon Tyne).

Overleaf: sunrise on Hadrian's Wall at Black Carts.

$\sim$7 Housesteads to Chesters

As one walks down the slope of Housesteads Fort, an important building, the communal latrine, is clearly visible in the left-hand corner (one wonders how many teachers with junior school parties rue the day that archaeologists successfully recovered the Hadrianic communal toilet block intact from the earth!). The land on which the fort was built inclines from north-west to south-east, so this was the only place for it: well-drained with efficient sluices and perfectly placed to carry the personal debris of 800 men well away from the fort where they lived and worked. It is to be hoped that the conduits outside the fort were as efficient as those within, as the *vicus* (civilian settlement) was clustered around the fort's southern walls!

The Housesteads *vicus* evolved into a substantial community in its own right, perhaps growing outwards from a nucleus around the well, located just outside the fort's curtain wall. Water played a significant part in some Celtic religious beliefs, and the Romans were tolerant about accepting new deities, so the well might have become the religious hub of both the military and civilian communities. Although only a handful of the civilian buildings remain exposed, more than twenty have been excavated, showing that merchants, artisans, tavern keepers and other essential camp followers lined the road connecting Housesteads with the Stanegate. Many other properties and strips of cultivated land were built on terraces due to the steepness of the site.

Opposite: the Wall snakes its way up to the summit of Sewingshields Crags. Although not quite the highest point on the Wall, its location overlooking Housesteads Fort and Broomlee Lough make it perhaps the most spectacular.

Right: excavated buildings immediately beyond the south gate of Housesteads Fort were part of the substantial civilian settlement that grew up to service the garrison.

Far right: a large communal well was set in the midst of what was the civilian workshop area to the south of the fort.

The easiest way to resume a walk along the Wall from Housesteads Fort is to head down the grassy slope leading away from the eastern flank and make for the Knag Burn Gate. An important crossing-point for civilian traffic, this was also an obvious target for cross-border incursions by native tribes seeking to exploit any weakness in the Roman defences. The views from the fort's northern wall are far-reaching, but descending to the valley floor at the Knag Burn Gate one gets a fuller appreciation of Housesteads' strategic importance. It was built on what is virtually the only large area of level ground on the eastern sector of the Whin Sill.

Well below the level of the fort, the stream was an invaluable source of fresh running water and some of the garrison's bathing facilities were located nearby. Fire was an ever-present risk in the relatively con-fined space of a walled garrison, so it made sense to locate bath-houses and their wood-burning water-heaters at a safe distance from the main fort.

The built-up section of the Wall ends shortly after the Knag Burn and is not encountered again until the upper reaches of Sewingshields Crags; it is replaced in the interim by a more recent boundary wall that twists and turns its way up to the summit. One short length of the original Roman Wall is just discernible in the springy turf near the end of the ascent, where the path swings round to the east to the trig point marking the elevation of Sewingshields Crags. From this exposed vantage point, the waters of Broomlee Lough (another glacial depression) can be seen almost directly below and, further on into the distance, the majestic sweep of hills and ridges bearing Hadrian's Wall.

Above: immediately east of Housesteads Fort, the valley of the Knag Burn created a natural north–south thoroughfare, and the gate established on the Wall became one of the major border control points.

Right: one of the more complete sections of Hadrian's Wall, on the summit plateau of Sewingshields Crags.

Overleaf: the view north-east from Sewingshields Crags reveals a bleak landscape populated by a few isolated farmsteads.

The north face of Sewingshields Crags is an almost unbroken line of severe rock faces and gullies, a natural defensive barrier that emphasises the importance of the few gaps created by natural faulting that appear at intervals along the length of the central Whin Sill. During the initial stages of the traverse across Sewingshields, the Wall's presence is intermittent; apart from one or two well-sustained sections, it is less impressive in stature than it is west of Housesteads. The scant outline of a demolished turret is passed on the descent from the trig point, but Milecastle 35 is the sole extant structure of any note. Its layout is reasonably well defined, although apart from one corner the walls scarcely extend above ground level.

The visible remains belong to the Roman period but the site was known to have been occupied in medieval times by a cluster of shielings. These were temporary settlements or buildings used by farmers and herdsmen during the summer, when they took cattle to graze on upland pastures. This ancient prac-

tice, known as transhumance, is common throughout Europe, especially in mountainous regions where harsh winters are the norm. The transfer of livestock is often marked by colourful processions and festivals. The name Sewingshields probably means a shieling belonging to Sigewine, a fairly common Anglo-Saxon name.

The sections of Wall flanking Milecastle 35 are substantial but their height is erratic. What remains is an excellent example of 'Consolidated' Wall, heavily cemented and pointed to prevent further disintegration. This is a poignant moment because, as the Wall ran down to the spinney behind Sewingshields Farm, it finally left the sanctuary of the inaccessible Whin Sill and became easy prey to those seeking a free source of ready-dressed stone. Just below the farm buildings lie the paltry walls of Grindon Turret. The National Trail path then crosses the B6318 to join the substantial banks and ditches of the *vallum* and progress east towards the fort of Carrawburgh (Brocolita).

Opposite, above: Milecastle 35 on Sewingshields might have been one of the Wall's more superfluous outposts, since the near-vertical, north-facing crags rendered any access from the north quite impossible.

Opposite, below: a section of consolidated 'Narrow' Wall built on 'Broad' Wall foundations on Sewingshields Crags.

Right: Grindon Turret (34A), immediately east of Sewingshields, had a short-lived tenure, being demolished towards the end of the second century; it was later used as a farm dwelling.

At first glance, this 1.5-hectare site, once occupied by an infantry fort, has little of interest to detain visitors long, with nothing to inspect other than grassy banks and ditches. But a large pay-and-display roadside car park suggests otherwise. A footpath leads round behind the fort to one of the Wall's hidden treasures, the Brocolita Mithraeum (Temple of Mithras). The fort was first excavated in the nineteenth century but the temple lay undiscovered until 1950, when a prolonged dry spell caused severe shrinkage of the surrounding earth and peat to reveal some of the temple's stones. The Persian sun god Mithras was one of the most popular deities worshipped in the Roman army, in a religion with complex initiation ceremonies and ascending ranks of attainment which appears to have been regarded as the exclusive preserve of officers. Mithraic temples

were dark and gloomy places, without windows, deliberately designed to replicate the cave portrayed in ancient sculpture in which Mithras is seen slaying a bull in ritual sacrifice, shedding its blood to fertilise the world.

Although the Wall itself is absent at this stage, one of the more enlightening sites is located a little further east at Limestone Corner. This was a civil engineering challenge rather than a military project. Where a natural barrier such as the Whin Sill did not protect the Wall's north side, the Roman engineers dug a forward ditch to run parallel with the Wall. At the end of a long, straight section, the trio of *vallum*, B6318 (originally the Wall) and ditch suddenly veers right to hug the landscape's contours. At the apex of the turn, a hollow where the ditch should be is littered with giant rectangular blocks of stone, many

Above: in contrast to the fort itself, the Mithraic Temple at Brocolita is an astounding relic of one of the Roman army's most favoured religious cults, that of the Persian god Mithras.

Opposite: the vallum at sunrise, looking towards Sewingshields Farm and Crags.

*Right: Limestone Corner is
remarkable for its scattered
piles of large stone blocks.
It marks the site where
the might of Roman
engineering gave in to
nature: when faced with
such an impenetrable layer
of rock, digging the Wall
ditch was abandoned.*

obviously cut earlier and somehow wrested from the
ground. It would appear that the builders were forced
to abandon the ditch here, due to an impenetrable
layer of hard rock.

One of the most agreeable sections of Hadrian's
Wall along this sector now follows; motorists who
have parked in the small lay-by to visit Limestone
Corner should pocket their keys and set out on foot
for the next few hundred metres. After leaving the
Roman rockery behind, the National Trail path
resumes the line of the Wall and gently descends
towards Black Carts, arguably the best of the few
remaining segments of Wall of any great length in
the final third of the journey to Wallsend. The Black
Carts Wall, obviously restored at some stage, is built
to full width and a good height, drawing one's eyes
upwards to wonder what a daunting spectacle the
original must have presented to friend and foe alike.

A minor road briefly interrupts the Black Carts
section of Wall before it continues onwards into a
field where the protruding remnant of a turret can
be clearly seen. In keeping with most of its contemporaries, Turret 29A was designed and built for the
'Broad' Wall. The Wall ends abruptly shortly after the
ruined turret, not even making it as far as the
boundary fence around the field.

Below: the line of the Wall and ditch on its gradual descent from Limestone Corner towards Black Carts.

Opposite: sunrise on Hadrian's Wall at Black Carts.

Above: the Wall at Black Carts is the last substantial section that will be encountered by walkers on the National Trail until reaching Heddon-on-the-Wall, some 25 kilometres further east.

Left: the surviving fragments of Black Carts Turret (29A).

Opposite: a retrospective view of the Wall at Black Carts with what was the old military road (now the B6318) running parallel to it right through to Greenhead at the western end of the Whin Sill.

After a brief climb, the route descends into the River North Tyne valley and the Roman cavalry fort of Chesters (Cilurnum). The country estate in which it stands was home to John Clayton, the man responsible for doing so much to preserve the Wall's priceless legacy (see Chapter 6).

Chesters was built to straddle the Wall and, as was customarily the case with cavalry forts, three of its four main gates opened to the north to enable a rapid response to any reported trouble. The Roman ruins were thoroughly excavated by John Clayton, after he had removed the hundreds of tons of earth placed over them by his father Nathaniel who had deemed them an unsightly intrusion into his otherwise perfectly laid-out eighteenth-century parkland! The site is extremely visitor-friendly, although care might be needed with small children as the bath-house is set almost directly above the North Tyne's west bank.

The bath-house is set slightly apart from the main complex, directly opposite the original bridge and almost immediately above the river's swirling waters.

Bath-houses were an integral part of Roman society and an essential component of any large garrison. The discipline of hygiene was regarded as an important element in military life, and a protracted bathing ritual was probably a useful antidote to boredom during off-duty hours.

Most of the barrack blocks and stables are represented by just a few token courses of stone, but the Commanding Officer's house retains a more substantial form. The building has been considerably modified over different periods of occupation; clearly discernible are the remains of its own bath-house, strong room and hypocaust heating system.

The perimeter of Chesters was additionally fortified by a tower at each corner and at regular intervals along the curtain wall. The civilian settlement that would have grown up in the shadow of the fort has yet to be excavated. Or perhaps it might be deemed better to let what remains of Nathaniel Clayton's original park rest in peace?

Above: the regimented lines of the garrison's main barrack blocks at Chesters Fort.

Above: the main bath-house at Chesters Fort has survived as an imposing ruin, whose walls rise to over 3 metres in places. It had the typical labyrinthine layout of many small rooms, each at different temperatures and varying degrees of humidity.

Left: the east gate of Chesters Fort is perhaps the most impressive, occupying a prominent position high above the river bank and almost directly opposite the Roman bridge abutment.

Below: a small collection of stunted pillars stands alongside the main barrack block walls at Chesters Fort.

~8 Chesters to Wallsend

Above: the bridge at Chollerford, a few hundred metres upstream from its Roman predecessor, replaced a medieval structure severely damaged by floods in 1771.

Opposite: the Wall and Roman bridge abutment opposite Chesters Fort, with the bath-house clearly visible on the opposite bank.

The final leg of the journey along Hadrian's Wall begins on the river's south bank, amid the remains of the Roman bridge abutment lying almost directly opposite the bath-house of Chesters Fort. Visitors wishing to inspect the site must cross the North Tyne on an elegant eighteenth-century replacement of earlier structures that were upgraded or rebuilt after floods. A solid footpath then runs parallel with the river, terminating at a small length of Wall that ran right up to the bridge which, in essence, was a continuation of the Wall.

During the post-Hadrianic phase of repair and reconstruction along other sections of the Wall, Chesters bridge was also rebuilt on a far larger scale. The new bridge was carried over the river on large piers, culminating in an even more substantial structure on the eastern side, incorporating a tower housing a water-powered mill. To the untutored eye, the bridge abutment might appear as just another cluster of stones, but looking back from the main road one cannot help but see the current bridge in a new light. The width of the river is probably different from what it was in the second century but, even so, the complexities of building a stone bridge become readily apparent — with hindsight, the Roman achievements are even more impressive.

The next accessible site after leaving Chesters and the river is Brunton Turret (26B) and the length of Wall into which it was incorporated. From a designated lay-by on the Chollerford to Wall road, a ladder-stile and kissing-gate lead up to a solid remnant of the Wall, comprising up to six courses of faced stone reaching a height of around 2 metres. The northern aspect of the Brunton Wall is now hemmed in by trees, but when first constructed it would have faced open ground. Perhaps the shelter provided by that band of mature trees has helped preserve the turret in such good condition; it is one of the most complete of those that have survived.

The turret's configuration shows that it was essentially a simple building with a sole entrance, intended for shorter-term occupation than the larger milecastles. Experts speculate about how turrets might have appeared when in use; based on pictorial references drawn from ancient sculpture, they could have extended to three storeys and been fitted with a covered walkway around the uppermost floor.

After a fairly steep climb out of the North Tyne valley, two significant sites lie in reasonably close juxtaposition (although on opposite sides of the road), part-way up Brunton Bank. The fragment of Wall at Planetrees is easy to miss; although it is in the care of English Heritage no signs herald its presence and there is only one place to park safely, which is unmarked. Planetrees, set in a field well below the level of the road, is visible only to westbound traffic; those heading uphill might need a couple of attempts to locate it but the reward more than outweighs any inconvenience.

Planetrees was the sole survivor of an early nineteenth-century onslaught on the Wall by local landowners keen to utilise its stones. It is lucky that this 15-metre length was not carted off to become the kitchen wall of a farmhouse, because it contains a fascinating junction of 'Broad' and 'Narrow' Wall, the latter clearly set upon the original full-width foundations. The saviour of Planetrees seems to have been one William Hutton who, in 1801, implored the landowner to spare the precious few remaining metres. Hutton was an early Alfred Wainwright prototype: at the age of 78, he set out from his home in Birmingham, walked to Carlisle, trudged along the entire length of Hadrian's Wall to the Tyne, and then walked back to the Midlands – a round trip of nearly 1,000 kilometres. He published an account of his journey the following year, entitled *The History of the Roman Wall*. I wonder if he smoked a pipe while walking, or was any good at drawing?

Above left: Brunton Turret (26B) and a 20-metre section of Hadrian's Wall are located on the gently rising slopes of the North Tyne valley, immediately east of Chollerford Bridge.

Above: the Wall at Brunton Turret (26B).

Opposite: the short, isolated fragment is one of the best examples of the 'Narrow' Wall being built on the substantial foundations already laid for the broader version.

There is less to see at Heavenfield, although a huge timber cross by the road and a church set in the middle of a nearby field give an indication that Christianity is somehow involved! The Battle of Heavenfield was fought in 635 AD between the forces of King Oswald of Northumbria and Cadwallon of Gwynedd, North Wales. Some explain this as a fight between Christian and pagan beliefs, but it was more likely to have been Anglo-Saxon *versus* Celt over territorial rights. The imposing cross is a twentieth-century version of one allegedly erected by Oswald on the night of the battle, around which he led his men in prayer. The eighteenth-century church occupies the site where that event was thought to have taken place.

Above: the view north from Hadrian's Wall at the Heavenfield battle site.

Right: a roadside cross on the B6318 east of Chollerford marks the site of the Battle of Heavenfield, fought in 635 AD between King Oswald of Northumbria and Cadwallon of Gwynedd: the 'home side' was victorious.

Opposite: a modern farm track now occupies the original course of the Roman Military Way south of the Heavenfield cross.

Above: the vallum at Port Gate near its junction with Dere Street. The Wall itself has disappeared at this point, but the vallum still cuts a swathe across the Northumberland countryside.

Above: Aydon Castle (English Heritage), a magnificent fortified manor house, is just a short distance south of the Wall near Corbridge. The site is not directly connected with the Roman period, but some of the stones within its substantial walls are.

Despite the *vallum's* almost constant presence, the road from Heavenfield is devoid of more tangible evidence of the Wall. The B6318 is checked briefly at its junction with the great north–south Roman highway, Dere Street; what was once an important border control point on the Wall, Port Gate, is now just another traffic roundabout. A worthwhile diversion to the Roman fort and town of Corbridge (Coria) can be made by turning right here and heading south down what is now the A68. This is not recommended for walkers: there are no footpaths and traffic can be fast and dangerous. Pedestrians would have a safer and more rewarding experience by charting their own route via bridle tracks and minor roads.

One such option passes by Aydon Castle, one of the country's finest examples of a fourteenth-century fortified manor house, naturally defended on three sides by the ravine of the Corr Burn. Corbridge is then easily accessed via an excellent public footpath that goes past the ominously named Gallows Hill and into the very heart of the Roman fort and town. Coria was first established during the Agricolan era as an important fort on the Stanegate–Dere Street crossroads. After the original fortified frontier line shifted northwards to the Wall, it evolved into a major settlement and supply base for the forward garrisons.

The Hadrian's Wall route along the B6318 can be rejoined back at Port Gate. The road continues to run in an almost unwavering straight line, and for good reason – it was built directly over the line of the Wall itself as a consequence of the 1745 Jacobite Rebellion. Charles Edward Stuart, 'Bonnie Prince Charlie', used General Wade's original military roads to march his forces rapidly down through Scotland to take Carlisle and progress south as far as Derby virtually unchecked. Meanwhile, the English army was, literally, bogged down between Newcastle and Hexham, unable to move artillery, troops or supplies across the country to counter the threat. In the aftermath, when blame was being apportioned, it was decreed that a similar disaster could never be allowed to happen again. So a new east–west military road was commissioned.

Hadrian's Wall was the obvious target, for two reasons: Roman surveyors had already charted the best course to adopt, and any remnants of the Wall and its foundations could be broken up to make an excellent hardcore base. The road that effectively destroyed some 50 kilometres of the Roman wall is attributed to General Wade; he might have instigated the planning process, but the actual construction did not begin until well after his death in 1748.

Opposite, above: Corbridge originated as a turf-built Stanegate fort, established in the first-century reign of Agricola. The ruined site visible today dates from its reconstruction in stone as a major supply base for the Wall garrisons. It is notable for its extensive and well-preserved granaries.

Opposite: a stone water tank from the Fountain House at Roman Corbridge.

Above: the eighteenth-century Military Road (now the B6138) was built over the 'arrow-straight' line of the Wall. In some places between Port Gate and Heddon, it survives as the only tangible evidence of Hadrian's legacy.

Above: Heddon-on-the-Wall is either the first or the last substantial section of the Wall to be encountered, depending on one's direction of travel.

Above: Denton Hall Turret (7B) and a few metres of the original 'Broad' Wall lie sandwiched between a main road and a housing estate on the outskirts of Newcastle.

Since departing from Planetrees, National Trail walkers will have had to content themselves with admiring the slowly passing countryside and playing a revised version of 'I Spy' called 'Spot the Vallum' to pass the time, until arrival at Heddon-on-the-Wall. There is a substantial length of 'Broad' Wall at Heddon but it has survived only to a modest and inconsistent height, seldom rising above just a couple of courses above ground. But it does provide an invaluable illustration of how wide the Wall might have been before construction plans were amended in favour of a narrower version. Unfortunately, this stretch does not coincide with a turret or milecastle, which would have significantly elevated the site's visual appeal.

Journey's end now starts to beckon. A few miles beyond Heddon, the line of the Wall becomes enve-

loped in the western fringes of Newcastle upon Tyne. One might assume that decades of urban expansion would have engulfed any remaining traces of Hadrian's Wall, yet three important sites have been saved and preserved, in the suburbs of Denton and Benwell. The first is easily located: Denton Hall Turret and a supporting length of 'Broad' Wall stand in a neatly railed-off green, immediately beside a main road into Newcastle. That the turret has survived at all is testimony to those individuals and organisations who fought for the protection and long-term care of such monuments, recognising their vital role as pieces in the complex jigsaw of our national heritage.

The remaining two sites, in Benwell, are less easily tracked down, being secreted in the midst of a suburban development of semi-detached houses and

bungalows. There can be few more incongruous sights than the Temple of Antenociticus surrounded by satellite dishes, dormer windows and washing lines. Any traces of the original fort of Benwell (Condercum) were swallowed up during the creation of a nearby reservoir and other buildings, but the temple, which lay to the south-west of the fort, has survived, albeit as little more than an outline. The deity to whom the temple was dedicated was a local Celtic god rather than one of the Roman army's 'regulars' such as Mithras or Jupiter. The stone altars gracing the temple today are replicas of originals removed after excavation (now in the Museum of Antiquities in Newcastle). This find was further confirmation that, in the pre-Christian era, any god could be worshipped if it was deemed capable of guaranteeing personal valour, victory in battle or more mundane services such as good harvests.

Also in Benwell is the *vallum* crossing, a complex arrangement of turf ditch and masonry which was probably typical of the other border checkpoints on the Wall; Benwell is the sole surviving example. The *vallum* would have been considerably deeper than it is now, and the metalled road that can clearly be seen approaching the gate really was the only way across the frontier for any form of wheeled traffic.

It is a shame that the National Trail guide makes no mention of these sites (even as an optional detour), but instead utilises an easily followed course along the banks of the River Tyne. The river is now stripped bare of heavy industry and, apart from one or two old quays and jetties, the walk is along a heavily restored waterfront. The centre of Newcastle has also undergone massive regeneration, and the only surviving traces of Roman occupation are the scant outlines of the fort, located within the confines of the twelfth-century castle. When bridged and fortified by the Romans during Hadrian's rule, Newcastle was known as Pons Aelius, after the Emperor's family name which is also borne by the bridge in Rome he built to provide access across the River Tiber to his mausoleum.

Wallsend (Segedunum) marked the eastern end of Hadrian's Wall. As might be expected, it boasted a substantial military presence housed within the customary playing card-shaped fort, encompassing about 2 hectares. The excavated site as presented today comprises ground-level outlines of all the principle buildings, a full-scale reconstruction of the bath-house, a visitor centre and a museum. A newly erected viewing tower offers comprehensive vistas over the fort and the Tyne, a panorama emphasising

Above left: the Benwell vallum crossing is the sole surviving example of a regulated crossing point with its attendant stone infrastructure.

Above: a diminutive temple dedicated to the little-known deity Antenociticus occupies a small green in Benwell, a western suburb of Newcastle. The original altars can be seen in the city's Museum of Antiquities.

Opposite: Newcastle's twelfth-century castle keep remains a historic landmark in an ever-changing city-centre skyline. It was built on the site of a Roman fort, traces of which are discernible in the castle's immediate environs.

the fact that Wallsend became one of the nation's main industrial areas. Most of the Roman site was buried beneath housing in the nineteenth century, and its excavation was a result of later industrial development. Had the nation's shipbuilding and mining industries charted a different course, Segedunum might still lie buried beneath bricks and mortar.

There are some who argue that Hadrian's Wall exists only where it can be experienced at first hand, along the Whin Sill ridge between Walltown and Sewingshields Crags. However, despite the absence of monumental remains in other places, only by travelling the entire length of the Wall can one fully appreciate the sheer scale of the undertaking, and wonder at the skill and tenacity of the legionaries who carried out their emperor's bidding.

It is perhaps as well that Hadrian built his Wall when he did, because there would be no chance of getting planning permission today!

Above: sunrise over the River Tyne from the National Trail route to Wallsend.

Left: the Wallsend Metro station has bilingual warning signs — in English and Latin!

Right: the National Trail continues towards Wallsend along the much-restored Tyne waterfront, where elegant modern architecture such as the Millennium Bridge blends harmoniously with the river's other famous bridges.

Left: adjacent to the site of
Segedunum, and where a
piece of the original Wall
has been excavated, a full-
size segment complete
with steps, walkway and
battlements has been built
to demonstrate how
Hadrian's Wall might have
appeared upon completion.

Above: the Roman fort of
Segedunum at Wallsend
may be represented by little
more than barely outlined
walls, but they are a
complete representation of
the original layout, backed
up by a state-of-the-art
Visitor Centre and
Museum.

Opposite: the ghosts of long-
departed legions and a
once-mighty shipbuilding
industry linger around
the deserted berths and
slipways of the River Tyne
at Wallsend.

Overleaf: the River Tyne
near Wallsend.

Useful organisations

Heritage, conservation & leisure

HADRIAN'S WALL
www.hadrians-wall.org
email: info@hadrians-wall.org
tel.: 01434 322002

ENGLISH HERITAGE
www.english-heritage.org.uk
email: customers@english-heritage.org.uk
tel.: 0870 333 1181

NATIONAL PARK
www.northumberlandnationalpark.org.uk
email: enquiries@nnpa.org.uk
tel.: 01434 605555

NATIONAL TRAIL
www.nationaltrail.co.uk/hadrianswall
email: nationaltrails@naturalengland.org.uk
tel.: 01242 533454

NATIONAL TRUST
www.nationaltrust.org.uk
email: enquiries@thenationaltrust.org.uk
tel.: 0844 800 1895

RAMBLERS ASSOCIATION
www.ramblers.org.uk
email: ramblers@ramblers.org.uk
tel.: 0207 339 8500

TOURIST INFORMATION
www.visitnortheastengland.com
www.visitgatesheadnewcastle.co.uk
www.golakes.co.uk

Principal sites & museums

TULLIE HOUSE MUSEUM & ART GALLERY
Castle Street, Carlisle CA3 8TP
www.tulliehouse.co.uk
tel.: 01228 618718

BIRDOSWALD FORT & VISITOR CENTRE
Cumbria CA8 7DD
2¾ miles west of Greenhead off B6318
www.english-heritage.org.uk/birdoswald
tel.: 016977 47602

VINDOLANDA & THE ROMAN ARMY
MUSEUM
Chesterholm Museum
Bardon Mill, Hexham NE47 7JN
www.vindolanda.com
tel.: 01434 344277

HOUSESTEADS ROMAN FORT & MUSEUM
Northumberland NE47 6NN
4 miles from Bardon Mill
www.english-heritage.org.uk/housesteads
tel.: 01434 344363

CHESTERS ROMAN FORT & MUSEUM
Northumberland NE46 4EU
¼ mile west of Chollerford on B6318
www.english-heritage.org.uk/chesters
tel.: 01434 681379

CORBRIDGE ROMAN SITE
Northumberland NE45 5NT
½ mile north-west of Corbridge on
minor road
www.english-heritage.org.uk/corbridge
tel.: 01434 632349

MUSEUM OF ANTIQUITIES
University of Newcastle upon Tyne
Newcastle upon Tyne NE1 7RU
www.museums.ncl.ac.uk
tel.: 0191 222 7844

SEGEDUNUM ROMAN FORT,
BATHS & MUSEUM
Buddle Street, Wallsend NE28 6HR
www.twmuseums.org.uk/segedunum
tel.: 0191 236 9347

ARBEIA ROMAN FORT & MUSEUM
Baring Street, South Shields NE33 2BB
www.twmuseums.org.uk/arbeia
tel.: 0191 456 1369

Index

1	2	3	4	5	6	7	8	9	10
11	12	13	14	15	16	17	18	19	20
21	22	23	24	25	26	27	28	29	30
31	32	33	34	35	36	37	38	39	40
41	42	43	44	45	46	47	48	49	50
51	52	53	54	55	56	57	58	59	60
61	62	63	64	65	66	67	68	69	70
71	72	73	74	75	76	77	78	79	80
81	82	83	84	85	86	87	88	89	90
91	92	93	94	95	96	97	98	99	100
101	102	103	104	105	106	107	108	109	110
111	112	113	114	115	116	117	118	119	120
121	122	123	124	125	126	127	128	129	130
131	132	133	134	135	136	137	138	139	140
141	142	143	144	145	146	147	148	149	150
151	152	153	154	155	156	157	158	159	160
161	162	163	164	165	166	167	168	169	170
171	172	173	174	175	176	177	178	179	180
181	182	183	184	185	186	187	188	189	190
191	192	193	194	195	196	197	198	199	200
201	202	203	204	205	206	207	208	209	210
211	212	213	214	215	216	217	218	219	220
221	222	223	224	225	226	227	228	229	230
231	232	233	234	235	236	237	238	239	240
241	242	243	244	245	246	247	248	249	250
251	252	253	254	255	256	257	258	259	260
261	262	263	264	265	266	267	268	269	270
271	272	273	274	275	276	277	278	279	280
281	282	283	284	285	286	287	288	289	290
291	292	293	294	295	296	297	298	299	300
301	302	303	304	305	306	307	308	309	310
311	312	313	314	315	316	317	318	319	320
321	322	323	324	325	326	327	328	329	330
331	332	333	334	335	336	337	338	339	340
341	342	343	344	345	346	347	348	349	350
351	352	353	354	355	356	357	358	359	360
361	362	363	364	365	366	367	368	369	370
371	372	373	374	375	376	377	378	379	380
381	382	383	384	385	386	387	388	389	390
391	392	393	394	395	396	397	398	399	400